Out of Control:

Cases of Debt-Collection Abuse in America…

…And What We Can Do About It

Bill Bartmann

Out of Control: Cases of Debt-Collection Abuse In America And What We Can Do About It

ISBN 978-0-983654-1-0-0

Printed in USA

Table of Contents

Introduction

I first saw the debt-collection industry long before I became a debt collector. I grew up in poverty, and more than once our family was evicted from houses that were condemned by the city for being "unfit for human habitation." I witnessed my parents being hounded by debt collectors until they eventually declared bankruptcy, and even then the browbeating did not stop.

Later in life I became the direct target of bill collectors on the other end of the phone when I was late on my payments. I experienced up close what it was like to be mentally raped by someone who was so practiced that there was no hint of hesitation in his voice.

You can learn more about me and my travels through the debt-collection industry elsewhere, but I have a more-important mission right now. I've become a collector of something else besides debts—I've collected dozens of stories in the press about my industry, and I want to share them with you.[1]

To an outsider reading the paper, these stories could seem unconnected and somewhat random. Because I'm in the industry, I see clear patterns of behavior. I also see the perverse incentives for many parties to abuse borrowers again and again.

Let's therefore take a tour of just a sample from my files about the cancerous part of the debt-collection industry—the part that feeds off unsuspecting citizens, destroys them, and moves onto ever-more victims.

Welcome to debt-collection hell.

---

[1]Note: I've condensed some of the stories for the sake of space, and also have put **key parts in bold face**. *My comments appear in italics.*

Part One:

An Epidemic of Debt-Collection Abuse

Problem #1: Some Industry Players—Including Some of The Biggest Ones—Are Simply Not Worried About Current Rules, or the Consequences of Violating Them.

Comment: It's already a violation of the Fair Debt Collection Practices Act to threaten borrowers. Nevertheless not only do some debt collectors do it, but they go to great lengths to become as creative in their threats as possible.

Also note in the following examples how we're not just dealing with one or two "bad apples", but with sometimes thousands of complaints against some of the major players in the industry.

#1: "You Better Kiss Your Daddy Goodbye."

Source:

WFTV Channel 9, Osceola County, Florida
http://www.wftv.com/countybycounty/24095998/detail.html

News Item:

An Osceola County couple says a debt collector went too far when he **told their 10-year-old daughter her father was going to be arrested.** The threat wasn't true and those types of threats are illegal.

The dad, who wants to be known as Mateo, is suing the collection company for harassment.

Mateo started saving the recordings after his collector called the house and his 10-year-old daughter answered the phone.

During the phone call, a man who identified himself as Officer Nick Anderson, but is a debt collector said, "Basically get ready to get arrested, goodbye."

Attorney Matt Englett says his firm has seen 500 complaints this year so far. He says the most common type of threat involves excessive phone calls, but he is seeing more and more cases like Mateo's.

"They told her, 'You better kiss your daddy goodbye. He's going to be arrested tomorrow or the next day,'" Mateo said.

#2: Collector Wants Sex for Repayment

Source:

My 9 News.WWOR-TV Channel 9 in New Jersey.Brenda Flanagan, investigator.
http://www.youtube.com/watch?v=WMdEO2lWDHg&feature=player_embedded#at=93

News Item:

"You know what **** means?

Why don't you tell Chris to come give me a quick ****....

You got no life. You're just a loser!

"Why don't you just go jump in front of a train? Why don't you do that? Get it over with y'know."

Later, in the same story, an item about a person named Nina, who was $15,000 in debt. This was the suicide note she wrote to her husband:

> "I'm so sorry. I really do love you, but I just cannot take this kind of pressure and humiliation."

She shot herself. Her psychiatrist said, "She had just been threatened with immediate jailing by credit representatives."

#3: "We'll Hang Your Dead Daughter from a Tree."

Source:

Chris Nagus, KMOV.com St. Louis
http://www.kmov.com/news/local/Foul-Mouth-Debt-Collectors--107059238.html

News Item:

Tammy Henshaw's daughter Angie died last May. She says she was unable to pay the funeral home $5,000 for the casket, the service, and use of the parlor. The funeral home entered a contract with Rumson, Bolling and Associates in California to collect Tammy's debt.

"They told me they were going to dig my daughter up and hang her from a tree," if she didn't pay the debt according to Henshaw. Henshaw says the calls came from the 818 area code, the debt collector confirms the phone number belongs to them.

Henshaw provided News 4 with a copy of the conversations she recorded. On the tape you hear a male voice making threats, you also hear the caller tell Henshaw she is "white trash." The caller goes on to say he's going to kill her dog and eat the animal, he also says he's going to send the sheriff to her home and have her arrested. Henshaw says the calls have caused emotional anguish, and she's even checked her daughter's grave to make sure it remains undisturbed.

#4: "Wouldn't It Be Terrible If Something Happened To Your Beautiful Daughter?"

Source:

Chris Serres and Glenn Howatt, Star Tribune staff writers
http://www.startribune.com/investigators/111727934.html

News Item:

Last year, a Texas collector with a criminal past telephoned Tosha Sohns, a Shakopee woman who owed money on a car. The collector said she had seen a photo of Sohns' "beautiful daughter" on MySpace. Then the collector asked, "Wouldn't it be terrible if something happened to her?" according to a lawsuit Sohns filed against the collections firm alleging harassment and invasion of privacy. The collector denied making the threat but admitted the rest.

#5: "Mean Pays."

Source:

ABC News Investigation by Brian Ross
http://www.youtube.com/watch?v=CZtqjMBlbY4&feature=related

News Item:

Brian Ross interviewed former star bill collector Mike Flanagan:

"I was not only Mr. Mean but I trained others on how to be Mr. Mean. When I first became a bill collector **I had absolutely no idea how ruthless and mean I could be, and for God's sake I was a U.S. Marine....**

Some people you can be completely polite and sweet to. Other people, you ram your fist down their throat and you pull the money out from their gullet. But you get the money."

#6: "We're Going to Hound You Until The Day You Die."

Source:

Paul Wenske, San Diego Union Tribune
http://www.signonsandiego.com/uniontrib/20051228/news_1b28debt.html

News Item:

The FTC sued Capital Acquisitions and Management Corp., claiming the national company pursued people without proof they owed anything and threatened some that if they didn't pay up "we're going to hound you until the day you die."

In court the trade commission called the business "a debt collection company gone wild." Steven Baker, director of the FTC's Midwest bureau, said: **"In many cases they had the wrong person, and we alleged they just didn't care."**

Attorneys for the company were unavailable to comment. The company has since gone out of business, and its millions of dollars in old debt have been liquidated and sold off to other debt buyers.

#7: "You'll Be Arrested By the MPs and Face a Dishonorable Discharge."

Source:

http://www.ag.ny.gov/media_center/2011/feb/feb18a_11.html

News Item:

Attorney General Eric T. Schneiderman today announced a series of actions against Buffalo-area debt collectors who preyed on military personnel and vulnerable consumers.

Stephanie Lowinger pleaded guilty to Scheme to Defraud in the 2nd Degree, a Misdemeanor. She is also permanently banned from engaging in any debt collection activities in New York State. Lowinger owned and operated Neiman, Rona & Associates, formerly Morgan Stone & Associates and later known as Gordon, Cappolli and Associates, all debt collection companies based in the Buffalo area.

This investigation found that Lowinger specifically targeted military personnel, referring to their alleged debts as "special accounts." Investigators discovered Lowinger said that **if payment was not made immediately, the active duty family member would be arrested by the military police and would face a dishonorable discharge.**

Lowinger and her debt collectors **falsely claimed to be lawyers, harassed consumers through repeated calls and abusive language, inflated the amount allegedly owned by debtor and levied unauthorized charges on the credit card accounts of consumers.**

#8: Threatens To Sexually Assault Daughter

Source:

CNN.com

http://www.cnn.com/2009/CRIME/08/21/debt.collection/index.html

News Item:

In a lawsuit filed this month in state supreme court in Erie County, [New York Attorney General Andrew] Cuomo's office alleges employees of 13 debt collection companies run by Buffalo-based Benning-Smith Group illegally **posed as law enforcement officials** or lawyers and **threatened to arrest and harm people** unless they made arrangements to pay.

In one case, a Benning-Smith collector **threatened to sexually assault a person's daughter if the person didn't pay the debt**, Cuomo's office said. In another, a collector told a woman that **he would pay the debt for her if she and her husband engaged in sex acts with him,** according to Cuomo's office.

The companies sometimes targeted people who owed nothing, Cuomo said.

"Some companies, for example, they have a debt from a John Brown, let's say. They go to the telephone directory and **they call all the John Browns with the same tactics, hoping that one of the John Browns will actually pay the bill**," Cuomo said at a news conference Wednesday in Mineola, New York.

"Many of these ... collection agencies, they buy the debt from an existing corporation and they use it as the basis to try to make collections. We have cases where **people didn't owe any money, but the tactics were so offensive yet so effective, they actually paid what the [collection agency] was asking just because they didn't want to deal with the phone call**," Cuomo said.

More than 850 consumer complaints against the group have been filed with Cuomo's office, the Federal Trade Commission and the Better Business Bureau, Cuomo's office said.

#9: "Child Protective Services Will Have To Take Your Kids."

Source:

CNN.com

http://www.cnn.com/2009/CRIME/08/21/debt.collection/index.html

News Item:

Michelle Minton was crying as she listened to a man tell her she'd be arrested within the hour if she didn't pay a $4,400 debt.

Michelle Minton says she was bullied into revealing her bank account number, though she didn't owe.

The man on the phone said he was a lawyer. Minton was at her Springville, New York, home with her children, ages 2 and 3, and her husband was away.

"[The caller] started talking about, **'Your kids will see you arrested**. If ... your husband can't make it home, **child protective services will have to take your kids**,' "she said, recalling the 2006 conversation.

Minton didn't owe anything, she says now. But feeling under pressure during that call, she gave the man her bank account number and she lost $900.

The caller, Minton alleges, wasn't a lawyer, but an employee of a debt-collection operation that New York Attorney General Andrew Cuomo is trying to shut down.

#10: 2:57a.m. Phone Call

Source:

ABC News Investigation by Brian Ross

http://www.youtube.com/watch?v=_dDArejnquI&feature=related

News Item:

Call from debt collector to laid-off executive about his car payment at 2.57am:

"This is the gentleman that was just at your door, who you refused to open the door and talk with?...and if you refuse to answer the door to me I guarantee you that I will wake up every neighbor in your entire ******* building, OK? And I'll let everybody know you don't know how to pay your bills. If someone knocks on your door, jackass, open it, you f***!"

#11: "I Will Find Her And I Will Find You And I Will **** You Up."

Source:

Jacksonville FL

http://www.news4jax.com/news/21578826/detail.html

News Item:

A message left on one local man's answering machine by a Jacksonville debt collector was laced with more than just profanity.

"Mr. -----, this is Mickey. When I see you I am going to **** you up," the collector says in a phone message. "I want my money and I want it now. My name is Mickey. I'm with Jacksonville ------. When I see you I will **** you up. ... I need my money. I will find your sister, your daughter, whoever Ms. Deborah **** is, but I will find her and I will find you and I will **** you up. Goodbye."

One debt collector called four times in a matter of just a couple of hours.

"Cupcake, I am like right now climbing into your family background," the debt collector said in a phone message. "I'm going to dig so deep up yours, you're going to wonder why you didn't do the right thing holding on to this vehicle making blank promises and trying to use me to do it. But that's OK. ... You're just another **** ****. Have a nice evening."

#12: Using Facebook To Find And Embarrass People

Source:

Tamara Lush, TheAssociated Press
http://www.washingtonpost.com/wp-dyn/content/article/2011/03/09/AR2011030903436.html

News Item:

A Florida judge has ordered a debt collection agency to not use Facebook or any other social media site in an attempt to locate a woman over a $362 unpaid car loan.

Judge W. Douglas Baird also ordered Mark One Financial LLC of Jacksonville, Fla. to refrain from contacting the woman's family or friends on Facebook.

The order is part of a lawsuit that Melanie Beacham filed last August against the debt collection agency. According to court documents, Beacham said Mark One **sent messages to her and her family on the Facebook networking site to have her call the agency about the debt.**

Billy Howard, the woman's attorney with the Morgan and Morgan law firm in Tampa, said the debt collectors violated Beacham's privacy. He said they also violated a provision of Florida's consumer protection law that prohibits debt collectors from harassing people.

Howard said that in the past four months, nearly a dozen potential clients have contacted him because debt collectors have used social media sites to track them down.

"It's the beginning of an epidemic," Howard said, calling it "another weapon" debt collectors can use.

Beacham's claims Mark One **contacted her six to 10 times a day by phone, sent her a text message, contacted her neighbor and sent a courier to deliver a letter to her workplace**, according to court documents. Mark One did not return a message Wednesday from The

Associated Press.

Last November, the agency said it would not discuss Beacham's case and denied any wrongdoing. The company acknowledged that its collectors use Facebook to find people when they don't respond to other means, like letters and phone calls.

Social media experts and lawyers like Howard say that debt collectors are increasingly trying new tactics to contact people who owe money.

In one Chicago case, **a man was friended on Facebook by a young woman in a bikini. The account turned out to be a debt collector's, something the man realized only when the "friend" posted a message on his wall: "Pay your debts, you deadbeat.**"

#13: 3,000 Complaints Against Just One Company

Source:

Paul Wenske, San Diego Union Tribune
http://www.signonsandiego.com/uniontrib/20051228/news_1b28debt.html

News Item:

Patricia Barnes got a letter in July demanding she pay nearly $6,500 – which included $3,500 in interest – on an old "Chase Providian" credit account. Never mind that she said **she never owned** a Chase or Providian card, much less a Chase Providian card, and that she has excellent credit after a 1992 **bankruptcy wiped out all her debts**.

But NCO Portfolio Management's letter informed the Topeka, Kan., woman it had bought the debt, supposedly going back 12 years or more. If she didn't pay up or respond in 30 days, the letter warned, she would be "subject to further collection" and the debt might be reported "to all national credit bureaus."

A boom in the multi-billion-dollar debt-buying industry has resulted in thousands of consumers getting dunned by **collectors trying to cash in on debts so ancient they are no longer enforceable in court or are beyond the seven-year period in which they can be reported to credit bureaus.**

Industry experts said …most debt buyers are ethical, with much of the negative publicity generated by a few bad apples.

The Federal Trade Commission…has found significant abuses in the collection of old, charged-off debt," said Joel Winston, the FTC's associate director for financial practices.

NCO Portfolio Management was one debt buyer sued, along with its parent, NCO Group Inc. In May 2004, NCO Group paid $1.5 million to settle FTC claims that inaccurate delinquency dates were affixed to consumer accounts.

As a result, **outdated debts – beyond the seven-year reporting period allowed by federal law – were reported to the three big credit bureaus, which can lower consumer credit ratings.**

Government records show that since the settlement, consumers have filed more than 3,000 complaints against NCO, many citing letters similar to the one Barnes received.

Records show the trade commission compiled more **than 400 pages dealing with complaints against NCO in August alone.** Complaints also have been filed with attorneys general in Missouri and Kansas, though most have been resolved, officials said.

NCO officials won't discuss the complaints but deny any wrongdoing.

#14: Man Surrenders Car So Mom Doesn't Go to Jail Over Husband's Funeral Expenses

Source:

Lisa Thompson, Credit and Collection News
http://www.creditandcollectionnews.com/viewer.php?url=http%3A%2F%2Fwww.goerie.com%2Fapps%2Fpbcs.dll%2Farticle%3FAID%3D%2F20110323%2FNEWS02%2F303239914%2F-1%2Fnewssitemap

News Item:

Howard D. Johnson III surrendered his car title to Unicredit America Inc. in 2008 because he feared the Erie debt collector was going to put his 73-year-old mother in jail for a debt she owed on her husband's funeral.

Erie County Judge Michael E. Dunlavey gave Howard Johnson permission to fight the $4,047 judgment that Unicredit entered against Johnson's then 73-year-old mother, Marilyn Johnson. Although Johnson was not a party to the litigation that resulted in that judgment, Dunlavey agreed that Johnson had an interest in the case because Unicredit had misrepresented debt-collection law. The judge also said Unicredit induced Johnson to make more than $2,000 in payments on his mother's behalf and surrender the title of his 2002 Chevrolet Cavalier.

None of the money Johnson paid to Unicredit had been turned over by Unicredit to the original creditor, Dunlavey noted.

Another hearing will be scheduled so that Johnson and his lawyer, Andrea Amicangelo of Northwest Legal Services, can argue that the judgment Unicredit filed against Marilyn Johnson should be struck. Johnson argued that because Unicredit improperly filed the judgment in Erie 6th Ward District Judge Dominick DiPaolo's court, even though the Johnsons' home and the funeral home are in Erie's 5th Ward.

Unicredit President Michael Covatto, who failed to appear at Unicredit's last court hearing, attended this morning's hearing. He said he had no lawyer and that he was trying to get together the funds to hire a lawyer to tell "the other side of the story."

He claimed to be ignorant of the claims the Johnsons are making against him. He also said that Lawrence D'Ambrosio, the lawyer who had filed the judgment for Unicredit against the Johnsons in 2008 and who had been served with the Johnsons' petition, had notified him of the hearing.

Covatto is scheduled to return to Dunlavey's courtroom this afternoon for a hearing in a separate matter -- the state Attorney General's ongoing lawsuit accusing the company of **using a fake courtroom and other tactics to fraudulently extract payments from debtors.**

#15: Purposefully Made Creditor Details Confusing So as to Delay Borrowers' Response

Source:

http://www.democratherald.com/news/local/article_bb01c14e-5100-11e0-9c4b-001cc4c03286.html

News Item:

A Eugene law firm that prompted complaints over its debt-collection tactics has to shut down under an agreement announced Thursday by Attorney General John Kroger.

The Justice Department started investigating Derrick McGavic and his partner Kristan Finney after getting more than 90 complaints about it from consumers, Kroger said in a press release from Salem.

McGavic & Finney specialized in representing national debt collectors that buy defaulted consumer obligations in massive quantities on the secondary market, often for pennies on the dollar.

Consumer complaints filed with the Oregon Department of Justice accused McGavic of ignoring debtor protections and rights afforded under the Oregon and Federal Debt Collection Protection Acts.

For example, McGavic allegedly misidentified or purposefully confused the identity of creditors in documentation to delay consumers' response and thus increase fees and interest payable to McGavic and his clients.

Notices issued by McGavic allegedly omitted specific information related to the amount of the defaulted debt and failed to provide proper verification of debts when requested by consumers. Similarly, McGavic allegedly repeatedly called debtors who had requested in writing not to be called.

The Department of Justice's investigation also uncovered McGavic's pattern of falsifying **fee affidavits in motions for default judgments by**

claiming services he did not perform. In addition, McGavic allegedly provided his office staff with a schedule to be used to arbitrarily increase the fees claimed — depending on the amount of money claimed or the venue of the action.

The agreement filed Wednesday in Lane County Circuit Court requires Derrick McGavic to pay $70,000 to the Oregon Department of Justice to reimburse the cost of the investigation; dissolve the law firm of McGavic & Finney, PC; and resign from the Oregon State Bar.

McGavic is further prohibited from acting as a debt collector or operating a law firm or a collection agency in the state of Oregon.

#16: Withdrew Funds And Charged Cards Without Customer Consent

Source:

Federal Trade Commission
http://ftc.gov/opa/2011/03/wam.shtm

News Item:

A leading debt collection company has agreed to pay a civil penalty of $2.8 million to settle Federal Trade Commission charges that its aggressive collection techniques violated federal law. As part of its efforts to protect consumers affected by the struggling economy, the FTC alleged that West Asset Management, Inc. violated the FTC Act and Fair Debt Collection Practices Act.

According to the FTC's complaint, **thousands of consumer complaints have been filed against West Asset Management Inc.**, which employs 1,500 debt collectors in 13 states and one offshore location. West Asset Management debt collectors allegedly violated the Fair Debt Collection Practices Act by calling consumers multiple times each day, often regarding accounts that did not belong to them, and sometimes using rude and abusive language. The FTC further charged that West Asset Management also illegally disclosed the existence of consumers' debts to third parties and **ignored consumers' written demands that West Asset Management stop calling them.**

The company also allegedly withdrew funds from consumers' bank accounts or charged their credit cards without consent and falsely claimed that consumers would be sued, arrested, or have their property seized for nonpayment of their debt. In addition, the FTC alleged that West Asset Management falsely claimed that partial payments would be accepted as full settlement on accounts and that negative information would stay on consumers' credit reports until debts were paid. According to the complaint, West Asset Management has collected on more than 24 million accounts on behalf of clients in the healthcare, telecommunications, consumer credit, and government service industries.

The settlement imposes a $2.8 million civil penalty, which is the largest civil penalty obtained by the FTC in a debt collection case. The settlement order permanently prohibits West Asset from using false, deceptive or unfair debt collection tactics.

Problem #2: How Easy It Is to Become a Debt Collector, No Matter How Checkered the Person's Background Might Be.

Comment: Many very fine people make careers in the debt-collection industry. They work hard to understand the borrowers' situations and help to find solutions.

However, the companies that take the "Mean Pays" attitude (see example #5 above) are also the ones that want to find the meanest, most unscrupulous people to hammer borrowers.

As you'll see in the next examples, they don't have to look far to find them.

#17: Criminals Land Jobs as Debt Collectors

Source:

Chris Serres and Glenn Howatt, Star Tribune staff writers
http://www.startribune.com/investigators/111727934.html

News Item:

Despite a Minnesota law, rapists, thieves, and other offenders are cleared to work as collectors -- with access to financial data.

Lee Song had already been caught forging checks when she swindled her former employer out of $127,122 by submitting phony payment vouchers.

Yet, less than four years later, the Minnesota Commerce Department cleared Song to work as a debt collector -- a job with access to people's private financial information.

Song is one of at least **743 criminal offenders in Minnesota who have been registered as debt collectors since 2005**, a Star Tribune investigation has found.

When offenders filled out state applications to be debt collectors, 75 percent of them lied about having a criminal past. The Commerce Department, which regulates collectors, **routinely approves criminals to work in the collections industry without conducting background checks**.

"The system in this state for screening collectors is broken," said Patrick Hayes, a consumer attorney in Minneapolis. "**These are people who can find out where you bank, where you live, even where your friends and relatives live, and the state doesn't seem to care if they are hardened criminals**. Why even register collectors if you register criminals?"

Their crimes include identity theft, rape, check forgery, assault, and most frequent, serious drunken driving offenses. Most offenders can legally work as collectors because state law excludes only those convicted of fraud or any felony within five years of their application.

Still, some collectors who shouldn't qualify because of their recent crimes are getting jobs. Since 2005, at least 111 registered collectors, including Song, had committed crimes that under state law should have barred them from debt collecting, according to the Star Tribune analysis of registration and court data. About a third of them still are registered as collectors.

Song, 32, went on an illegal shopping spree after the state approved her application to work at Receivables Management Solutions, a collections firm in West St. Paul. She ordered $1,561 in jewelry, car repairs and food using credit card numbers stolen from people she telephoned about unpaid debts. When police in April led Song away from the call center, it was the fourth time in nine years she was arrested for a financial crime.

The department said it reviews the criminal records only of those who check the box admitting to past crimes, or when the department receives information suggesting someone has a criminal history. **Criminals who lie don't get a background check.**

One in 12 debt collector applicants cleared to work in Minnesota call centers since 2005 had criminal records in the state. And 120 of the 743 offenders were registered more than once.

With so much data at their fingertips, unscrupulous collectors can wreak havoc on people struggling with unpaid bills.

Debt collectors often have access to Social Security numbers and use "skip tracing" tools to identify a person's employer, unpaid loan balances, phone numbers, home address and relatives. They also prowl the Internet.

#18: Would You Give Them Your Credit Card Number?

Source:

http://www.startribune.com/investigators/111728189.html
Minnesota Commerce Department and court records.

News Item:

Minnesota law says people convicted of fraud or any felony are barred for five years from working as debt collectors. The job gives them access to private financial data, including credit card numbers. Offenders routinely lie to get around the law.

Joseph J. Benitz, 31

A former debt collector who now works as a repossession agent, Benitz was convicted of misdemeanor criminal property damage in 1998. In a personal feud, he bashed a car with a crowbar while two terrified people were inside. A year later, he added disorderly conduct to his record after confronting a woman at her apartment with a baseball bat. In 2001, he was convicted of fleeing a police officer in a car and on foot. He needs no license to repossess vehicles.

Keisha R. Burrus, 33

She got her first job in debt collection after being convicted of misdemeanor theft in 2001 for stealing someone's identity and using it to obtain credit and buy expensive jewelry. Burrus remained a debt collector, most recently at AllianceOne, even after her felony theft conviction for carting $1,634 in stolen goods out of a Target store.

Sherria E. Mustin, 26

In 2005, she stole a former friend's identity and used it to charge a $1,460 computer online. While the swindling charges were pending in court, she went to work for a new collections company. That required her to fill out a new state debt collector registration form. She checked "no" where it asked if she had ever been charged with a crime. In 2007, she was convicted of felony check forgery for persuading a co-worker at a collections firm to cash counterfeit traveler's checks at banks, pocketing $1,029.

Zachariah D. Hankel, 28

Hankel has applied for or renewed his state debt collector registration three times since 2003, and currently works for a collection company in Roseville. State records show a 2003 conviction for felony receiving stolen goods. The records also show he was convicted of felony domestic assault in 2005 and spent a year in prison for repeatedly hitting a former girlfriend, whom police found bleeding in a hotel lobby.

Joseph L. Berntsen, 28

Berntsen's career as a debt collector could be over. He's back in jail after violating probation on a 2006 felony conviction for sexually assaulting a woman in Braham, Minn. He says he was recently dismissed by Financial Recovery Services Inc. of Edina for not collecting enough money. The Commerce Department last week still had him registered as a collector.

Sara A. Legros, 24

In 2009, she stole someone's PIN number and gave it to an acquaintance to get cash from an ATM for drugs, court papers say. She pleaded guilty to financial transaction card fraud, and the felony was reduced to a misdemeanor in court. Around the same time, Legros acted as a "lookout" during a home burglary, and drove away in a stolen car, resulting in another misdemeanor conviction, court papers say.

#19: State's Largest Debt Collector Failed To Conduct Criminal Background Checks On Collectors

Source:

Chris Serres, Star Tribune

http://www.startribune.com/business/114767304.html

News Item:

Minnesota Commerce Commissioner Mike Rothman put a number of the state's largest debt collection firms on notice this week that he is prepared to take disciplinary action against them for allegedly **failing to conduct criminal background checks on individual collectors**.

The eight debt collection firms put on notice include Allied Interstate Inc. of Plymouth, AllianceOne Receivables Management Inc. of Eagan, Bureau of Collection Recovery of Eden Prairie, I.C. System Inc. of St. Paul, Financial Recovery Services Inc. of Edina, NCO Financial Systems Inc. of Mendota Heights, Receivables Management Solutions Inc. of West St. Paul, and Van Ru Credit Corp. of Des Plaines, Ill.

In separate consent orders, Rothman advised the firms that he is "prepared to commence formal action" against their licenses based on allegations that the firms failed to adequately screen individual collector applicants before submitting registration applications.

The firms were told that they may resume registering individual debt collectors after the state commerce commissioner completes a review of their screening process.

A Star Tribune investigation recently found that **collectors in Minnesota routinely lie about their criminal backgrounds in order to get work in industry call centers. Their crimes include identity theft, rape, check forgery, assault, and drunken driving offenses.**

The investigation found that **one in 12 debt collector applicants cleared to work in Minnesota call centers since 2005 had criminal**

records in the state.

Since 2005, the state Commerce Department has fined at least five collections firms for inadequate screening of new hires.

Problem #3: Some Debt Collectors Pursue Ancient Debts That Have Been Dormant For Years and In Fact Are Older Than the Statute of Limitations.

Comment: They go by terms like "zombie debt" and "time-barred debt", but whatever you call them, they're very old debts that have passed the statute of limitations for borrowers to be sued on.

Crooked debt collectors find such limits not to be a problem, because they have a great solution: Just persuade borrowers to make a payment—any size of payment—on the debt. What they don't tell them is what happens when they make that payment, as you'll see in the examples below.

#20: Borrowers Make Small Payments On Post-Statute Debt Unaware That It Starts The Clock Again

Source:

Chris Serres, Star Tribune

http://www.startribune.com/politics/state/83980787.html

News Item:

For years, Minnesota has been known for having one of the friendliest climates in the nation for companies that profit from buying and collecting old consumer debts.

But that could soon change if two state legislators have their way and the Minnesota Legislature goes along.

A draft bill to be introduced later this month would require debt buyers filing collection lawsuits to produce an assortment of documents proving that borrowers being sued actually owe the unpaid debts. The proposed legislation would **also ban a practice known as "re-aging," in which debt buyers try to collect on old debts. Under current law, debt collectors can renew long-delinquent debts -- even when the statute of limitations has expired -- by persuading consumers to make small payments, which renews the default date.**

The bill would make it impossible for debt buyers to revive a statute of limitations by collecting on an old account. Any legal action must also include a signed affidavit stating the debt has not passed the statute of limitations.

But some consumer attorneys say the bill does not go far enough in addressing this state's relatively friendly laws on debt collection. **Minnesota is one of just a handful of states that allow collections firms to initiate a lawsuit against a debtor simply by serving a summons and without actually filing documents with the court -- a practice known as "hip pocket filing." Many consumers are unaware they have been sued until it's too late, and the collections firm has**

won a default judgment.

But the law likely would have helped Philip Doroff, 28, of New Hope, who said he was sued by a debt buyer a year ago for a Capital One credit-card debt of $650 that he thought he repaid. When he contested the lawsuit in court and asked the firm for evidence, the firm produced an unsigned Capital One credit-card agreement from 2004 -- even though he got the card three years earlier.

Ultimately, Doroff prevailed in court, but only after spending $3,000 in legal bills. "The case should never have gone to court," he argued, "because they never had legitimate information. ... Having to prove that this is what you actually owe should not be a radical proposition."

#21: Re-Activating Time-Barred Debt

Source:

Sara Murray, Wall Street Journal
http://online.wsj.com/article/SB10001424052748704754304576096132208528542.html?mod=WSJ_WSJ_US_News_5

News Item:

"One of the abuses in the debt-collection industry was debt collectors who would misrepresent to people what the risks were about very old debt," said Jonathan Mintz, commissioner of the New York City Department of Consumer Affairs. "People can make old debts fresh again by making partial payments."

The Federal Trade Commission has urged states to take a harder line on collecting old debts.

"Consumers are not aware that collectors cannot lawfully sue to recover on time-barred debt," the FTC said in July.

Problem #4: It's Far Too Easy for Major Corporations to Sue for Debt Collection

Comment: The whole idea behind small-claims court has always been for two parties with roughly similar resources to come together and resolve a matter quickly. For instance, my clothing was ruined at your dry cleaners, and we're going to court to see how we can resolve the issue. Here's how California describes it:

> *"Small claims court is a special court where disputes are resolved quickly and inexpensively. The rules are simple and informal."*[2]

That's not how it's working out for hundreds of thousands of people around the country. One of the original benefits—a court in which you can file a suit inexpensively—has recently been hijacked by large corporations. They robo-file tens of thousands of suits with a push of a button and in some cases with no proof necessary.

The problem goes well beyond just how easy it is to robo-file lawsuits. It also extends to how defendants are not effectively notified of the court dates, and what happens when they don't show up—or even when they do, as you will see.

Read the following examples and decide for yourself if the system seems to be fair for all parties.

---

[2]http://www.courtinfo.ca.gov/selfhelp/smallclaims/scbasics.htm

#22: Just $40 to File a Lawsuit

Source:

Boston Globe

http://www.boston.com/news/special/spotlight_debt/part2/page4.html

News Item:

At Boston Municipal Court, the state's busiest small-claims court, roughly **85 percent of the lawsuits are brought by companies collecting old debts**, according to Kevin F. Callahan, first assistant clerk-magistrate for the civil division. The downtown court has handled 40,000 small claims in five years; it gets so many suits from Norfolk Financial, Commonwealth Receivables Inc., Filene's, and NStar that it had ink stamps made for each one.

At a cost of **just $40 to file a lawsuit** for any amount up to $2,000, debt collectors find a bargain in Massachusetts small claims. **A victory in court lets them pursue a debt for up to 20 years, and earn 12 percent annual interest on it** - a rate that's matched or exceeded in only five states. The Legislature hasn't adjusted that rate since the 1980s.

"We're sophisticated collection agencies for these people," Callahan said. "This is a lucrative business for some. ..... I hate it."

#23: Computer-Automated, High-Volume Litigation

Source:

June Williams
http://www.courthousenews.com/2010/11/15/31828.htm

News Item:

A Bellevue [Washington] law firm works with collection agencies to mislead courts and consumers by using "robo-signers" in Minnesota who sign up to 400 affidavits a day, falsely swearing they have "personal knowledge" of cases in Washington state, to secure speedy default judgments, according to a federal class action.

The class claims that Encore Capital Group, Midland Funding, and Midland Credit Management work with the Suttell & Hammer law firm, faxing a boilerplate form to a "legal specialist" in Minnesota, who signs the affidavit before any supporting documents are attached.

"Encore Capitol Group ('Encore Capitol') has developed a proprietary, sophisticated, 'system driven' collection process based on the 'predictive behavior' of consumers (and state courts). In conjunction with its subsidiaries and 'franchisee' law firms (including the Suttell Law Firm) it engages in **computer automated, high volume, state court litigation** in the collection of distressed debt (purchased at pennies on the dollar).

"That predictive behavior results in a very high default rate of judgments of unproven cases or for inflated amounts: 1) because the filing of the collection lawsuit by an attorney implicitly misrepresents that the attorney has had meaningful involvement in developing and evaluation of the case against the consumer-debtor, 2) because consumer-debtors frequently default if it is made to appear that a creditor, represented by an attorney rather than a collection agency has sued them, and 3) because that state courts reviewing high volume filings of defaults and summary judgments will enter judgments if it appears on the surface that documentation supporting the debt has been properly attached to the default or summary judgment package. The debt collectors collecting purchased distressed debt have a significant hurdle to overcome in the collection of large portfolios of distress debt (much of it aged) using the state courts. Due to the nature of the purchased distressed debt, the high volumes, and automation the defendants are unable to meet the requirements of the rules of evidence of providing proof of the records of the debt without misleading the state courts and consumer debtors.

"Instead of providing actual admissible evidence of the proof required in a breach of contract lawsuit, the Encore defendants (with the knowledge of the Suttell attorney defendants) hire collection agency employees as 'Robo-signers,' according to the complaint. "The Robo-signers sign several hundred affidavits a day falsely claiming that they are a business records custodian with personal knowledge of the facts. They falsely claim in the affidavit knowledge of the assignment(s) of the debt, the amount of the debt, the interest rate, the default of the debt, the alleged credit card terms and conditions, and the record keeping procedures of every bank in America.

"It is made to appear to the state court judges that the debt records filed with the court were attached to the affidavit by the affiant. This is not true. The affidavits are signed in Minnesota by a Midland Credit Management (a licensed collection agency) employee. Only the two (2) page affidavit is shipped to the Suttell Law Firm in Bellevue Washington. A non-attorney Suttell employee sometime later, as needed, selects and attaches documents to the 'business records affidavit' to send to the court for filing whenever a default or summary judgment motion is required. The court is lead to believe that the affiant has authenticated and established the reliability of the records but the affiant does not even know what records will be later attached to the affidavit by the Suttell employees."

The complaint adds: "The affidavit is printed on a printer at the desk of a randomly selected MCMI employee, employed in St. Cloud, Minnesota. **The person selected to sign the affidavit is based upon when the affidavit comes off the printer and which printer rather than any personal knowledge of the affiant of the account being collected."**

The class claims that each "legal specialist" signs 100 to 400 affidavits a day. **One specialist who swore she had personal knowledge that "the plaintiff's predecessor in interest sold and assigned all right, title and interest" did not "have any personal knowledge of who the plaintiff, Midland Funding LLC's predecessor in interest was or even know what a 'predecessor in interest' was,** nor what it means to have 'sold and assign all right title and interest,'" according to the complaint.

Defendant Midland Funding is wholly owned by defendant Midland Portfolio Service, which is owned by defendant Midland Credit Management, which is owned by defendant Encore Capitol Group. All work out of the same address in San Diego.

The class claims false affidavits were "served and filed in thousands of cases," in violation of the Fair Debt Collection Practices Act, the Washington Consumer Protection Act and the Washington Collection Agency Act.

#24: Suits Against People Because Their Names Are Similar

Source:

David Shaffer, Star Tribune

http://www.startribune.com/business/118777379.html

News Item:

The Minnesota Attorney General went to court Monday seeking to halt one of the nation's largest debt collection firms from a systematic practice of "robo-signing" court affidavits resulting in allegedly false and deceptive lawsuits to be filed against consumers across the country.

A lawsuit against Midland Funding LLC, a San Diego-based company that buys old consumer debt from credit card companies and others, said its employees in St. Cloud signed affidavits falsely stating they had proof of consumers' debts. Then **Midland filed collections lawsuits against people who already had paid what they owed as well as people whose names were similar to the actual debtors.**

The company is one of the state's biggest filers of lawsuits, with 15,000 cases in Minnesota alone since 2008. Across the country, **it filed 245,000 consumer lawsuits** in 2009 to collect, the attorney general said.

But Attorney General Lori Swanson said Midland workers routinely don't verify that consumers actually owe money on an old debt. Instead, she said, the company mass produced affidavits about alleged debts based on information in databases of debts as much as 10 years old and submitted to courts as proof.

In some cases, consumers didn't even know they were being sued because Midland claimed to have served court papers where they no longer lived. When consumers didn't respond, the company was able to obtain judgments against them.

"The company put its thumb on the scale of justice to unfairly tilt the collection process in its favor," Swanson said at a press conference announcing the lawsuit.

She said it is the first time a consumer enforcement lawsuit has been filed over debt collection robo-signing, though the practice that has been widely criticized in foreclosure cases. Robo-signing is the practice of signing legal documents and attesting to them as being true even without reading them or verifying the information.

It was not clear how many false lawsuits allegedly have been filed based on robo-signed documents, she added. The lawsuit seeks fines of $25,000 per violation under state and federal debt collection laws.

Midland and its publicly-traded parent corporation, Encore Capital Group, Inc., are part of the booming debt buying industry. They purchase electronic databases of billions of dollars of old, charged-off consumer debt from credit card companies, banks, telecommunications firms and others.

Midland and Encore have paid more than $1.8 billion to obtain 33 million customer accounts with a face value of about $54.7 billion, or an average cost of about three cents on the dollar, Swanson said.

Deputy Attorney General Nate Brennaman said the company receives just one line of data on each debtor, including the name, an address and the amount. Midland does not rely on other original documents obtained from banks and creditors to verify the debt, he said. The lawsuit was served on the company and filed in a federal court in Ohio, where a class-action lawsuit is underway against Midland.

Note: Encore owns Midland. Here's what Encore says about affidavits in its "Consumer Bill of Rights":

ENCORE
CAPITAL GROUP

mcm
midland credit management, inc.

Article 6: The Fair and Reasonable Use of Litigation to Resolve an Outstanding Obligation

a. Prior to pursuing a collection strategy that may include litigation, we will attempt to contact the consumer to let them know that the next step in the collection process will be their referral to a law firm.

b. We will engage law firms that litigate in good faith and treat consumers with respect.

c. Prior to signing affidavits, our authorized representatives will read, understand, and fully verify document contents as appropriate to ensure accuracy. All notarized documents will be signed in the presence of a certified notary who is acknowledging the signature.

#25: One Person, 40,000 Affidavits

Source:

http://blogs.forbes.com/danielfisher/2011/01/04/judge-allows-rico-suit-over-debt-collection-tactics-to-proceed/

News Item:

A federal judge in New York has rejected attempts by Leucadia National and the debt-collection law firm Mel Harris & Associates to dismiss a class-action lawsuit accusing them of a racketeering scheme to obtain judgments in New York courts against unwitting consumers around the country.

In the ruling issued Dec. 29, U.S. District Judge Denny Chin said the plaintiffs could proceed with claims they were the victims of a "sewer service" scheme in which process servers fraudulently told the court they'd presented debt-collection papers to their targets as required under the law. The lawsuit on behalf of up to 100,000 borrowers claims lawyers at Mel Harris then used those statements to obtain default judgments against the consumers and threaten to garnish their wages or freeze money in their bank accounts. The customer for these services was Leucadia, a financial-services firm that bought hundreds of thousands of defaulted debt claims for pennies on the dollar and hired Mel Harris to recover what it could.

The suit has echoes of the "robosigner" controversy over home mortgages, but with important differences. Mortgages are loans secured by a physical property, so there's rarely any dispute over what the homeowner owes and what the lender can seize if he doesn't pay.

Leucadia was trying to collect on unsecured debt, where there is no collateral and little recourse for the lender. **To get judgments against the borrowers, the judge said, a single Mel Harris employee named Todd Fabacher signed 40,000 affidavits attesting to the accuracy of debt claims.**

Assuming 260 business days a year, Fabacher had to have personally (and purportedly knowledgeably) issued an average of twenty affidavits of merit per hour, i.e., one every three minutes, over a continuous eight-hour day.

Mel Harris has drawn attacks from consumer advocates over its debt-collection practices, which include **filing more than 100,000 lawsuits** in state courts around the country. The Federal Trade Commission has expressed concern about debt collectors who obtain default judgments against consumers who were never told of the lawsuit against them and never appeared in court. The term "sewer service" refers to the practice of throwing service papers in the sewer but telling the court the target received them in person.

#26: Court Papers Sent To Address Where the Person Hadn't Lived For 23 Years

Source:

David Shaffer, Star Tribune

http://www.startribune.com/business/118777379.html

News Item:

Employees at a giant debt collection company in St. Cloud "robo-signed" thousands of collection documents without verifying their accuracy, allowing false and deceptive lawsuits to be filed across the country against consumers who didn't owe money, the Minnesota attorney general charged Monday.

The state lawsuit against Midland Funding LLC, one of the nation's largest debt collection firms, is the first enforcement action in the country against a debt collector for robo-signing, Attorney General Lori Swanson said.

Midland workers admitted signing up to 400 affidavits a day without reading them or verifying whether a debt was owed, according to the lawsuit. Often, the debts were 10 or more years old, known as "zombie debt," that Midland had purchased for cents on the dollar from credit card companies and other businesses, Swanson said.

"**This company has a history of targeting people and assuming they owe them money until the citizen can show they don't owe the money**," said Swanson, appearing at a capitol press conference with five Minnesotans who had been subjected to the practice.

"It really flips the process on its head because a debt collector or a debt buyer shouldn't be targeting anybody for payment of a bill unless they substantiate that a person actually owes the money," Swanson said.

Midland is one of the state's biggest filers of lawsuits, with 15,000 cases in Minnesota alone since 2008. Across the country, the debt collector filed 245,000 consumer lawsuits in 2009, Swanson said. The company also has offices in Arizona, Texas and India.

Debt buyers receive just one line of data on each debtor, including the name, an address and the amount, Deputy Attorney General Nate Brennaman said. When purchasing debts, Midland and other companies do not purchase underlying charge slips and contracts to prove money is owed, according to the lawsuit.

Daniel Fischer of Brooklyn Park said he discovered he had been a victim of Midland's tactics a year ago, when his credit card company reduced his credit limit because of a "derogatory statement" in his credit report. It turned out that Midland had sued him five years earlier, obtained a judgment for $1,155 and was ready to garnish his paycheck or other assets.

But Fischer didn't owe anyone money, and **the order to appear in court to prove his innocence was sent to an address where had hadn't lived for 23 years**. Only after he contacted the attorney general's office did Midland's law firm, Messerli & Kramer of Minneapolis, drop the case, he said.

That pattern was repeated with Barbara Thies of Eagan, who kept getting dunned for an obligation she had paid before it was due in 2001. **Thies said she repeatedly sent the canceled check to Midland, but had to go to court anyway.** There, confronted with the evidence in person, the Messerli firm dropped the case in 2007, she said.

But that didn't repair her credit. Later, her auto and home insurers raised her rates because her credit rating had dropped, she said. She does not believe the company simply made a mistake.

"I think they are predatory," Thies said of Midland. "This is a choice. They clearly know they are doing this. This isn't an error in judgment. I think this is a business model."

The state lawsuit includes partial transcripts of interviews with three Midland employees who signed collection affidavits, including Elizabeth Ann Neu of St. Cloud.

"Did you ever read the affidavit all the way through?" an attorney asked her.

"No," replied Neu.

Neu, reached by phone, said she left the company a year and a half ago. She declined to comment further.

Swanson said consumers who don't respond to mailed legal notices often don't realize that debt collectors can easily obtain a default judgment. Some consumers subjected to Midland's tactics said they wondered if the phone calls and mailings were a scam.

#27: Major Problems with Court Notifications

Source:

Boston Globe

http://www.boston.com/news/special/spotlight_debt/part2/page4.html

News Item:

In Massachusetts, notices of lawsuits are sent by first-class mail to the address supplied by collectors. **Often these addresses are out of date, yet the courts assume the defendant was notified unless the letter is returned.** This is a flawed system, the Globe found in a test: **Of 100 letters sent to the same person at incorrect addresses across the state, just 52 came back marked "return to sender" by the post office; the other 48 simply went missing.** A backup requirement that debtors receive notice by certified mail was dropped two years ago as a cost-saving measure.

Even when properly delivered, **the notice sent to defendants would confuse almost anyone.** The debtor's instructions are listed in tiny, faint type on the back of the form, and are in many ways misleading. For example, they say that plaintiffs must prove their claims - something that never occurred during the many hearings attended by the Globe. They also **fail to warn defendants of the serious consequences of failing to appear**: The collector automatically wins, gaining the right to seize property, garnish wages, put a lien on a home, or get a civil arrest warrant to have the defendant hauled into court.

Even defendants who do show up tend to lose most of the time, and for a simple reason - they owe the money, or at least part of it. But **many cases that could be contested are not**. With a little information, and pluck, lawyers say, many defendants could turn the tables against the collectors by demanding that they produce evidence of the debt.

"You have rights, too. It's not just the creditor," said Joseph B. McIntyre, a collection lawyer in New Bedford. "But you've got to be brave enough to vindicate your rights."

#28: A Dead Person Reviewed Your Case

Source:

Wall Street Journal
http://online.wsj.com/article/SB100014240529702042040045760499021
42690400.html

News Item:

She died in 1995. Yet her signature later appeared on thousands of affidavits submitted by one of the nation's largest debt collectors, Portfolio Recovery Associates Inc., in lawsuits filed against borrowers.

Some regulators complain that the use of Ms. Kunkle's name reflects an epidemic of mass-produced, sloppy and inaccurate documentation in the debt-collection industry. Lawsuits have surged as more borrowers fall behind on payments and collection firms turn to courts to get what they are owed.

After being sued for fraud, Portfolio Recovery Associates decided in early 2008 that any documents bearing Ms. Kunkle's name had "defects" and shouldn't be used when trying to collect debts, a company spokeswoman said.

Last July, though, lawyers for Portfolio Recovery Associates sought a court judgment in a lawsuit against a Seattle woman for $2,892.10 in credit-card debt and interest that she allegedly owed. It was a cookie-cutter case, except for one thing: To vouch for the debt's validity, the Norfolk, Va., company included an affidavit signed by Martha Kunkle.

In 2008, Judy Montoya, an employee at Portfolio Recovery Associates, testified in a debt-collection suit filed by the company that its "legal specialists" sign as many as 200 affidavits a day. The company's spokeswoman said such employees sign an average of 100 affidavits a day and are guided by "a very rigorous set of policies and procedures." Ms. Montoya couldn't be reached to comment.

Concerns about Ms. Kunkle's affidavits were raised in 2008 by lawyers for Jeanie Cole, one of thousands of Montana residents sued by Portfolio Recovery Associates to collect debts. After failing to locate Ms. Kunkle, lawyers for Ms. Cole interviewed her daughter, who worked at Providian in a document-processing division.

The daughter testified in a deposition that other Providian employees used the name Martha Kunkle when signing affidavits. Along with other employees, the daughter was responsible for signing affidavits.

The lawsuit against the Seattle woman included an October 2006 affidavit in which "Martha Kunkle, Designated Agent" for Providian, swore "to the best of my knowledge" that the amount owed "reflects a true and correct accounting of the cardholder's credit card account."

#29: Guilty Until Proven Innocent

Source:

http://www.startribune.com/investigators/101723868.html

News Item:

After two weeks without a decent meal, Van Tran looked tired and agitated as he walked into the Ramsey County courtroom for a hearing in May.

Tran, 55, a janitor and security guard from St. Paul, had waited for this chance to explain why a collections firm made a serious mistake when it seized $8,016 from his bank accounts -- three years' worth of savings -- to collect an alleged Discover credit card debt. Tran held a police report showing he was a victim of identity theft.

"I just want my money back until this is resolved," Tran, a Vietnamese immigrant, recalls pleading to Judge Thomas Mott. "I need money to eat."

But speedy justice was denied Tran, as it is for many debtors whose savings or paychecks are seized in a legal process called garnishment.

At nearly every stage of the process, **the deck is stacked against consumers**. In Minnesota, unlike most states, collectors can start a lawsuit without filing anything in court. If a consumer doesn't respond, they can seize bank accounts or part of a paycheck. Most states require judicial oversight. But in Minnesota, collectors can take people's money without proving in court the debt is owed.

The bad economy and the rapid growth of a new industry that collects old debts once deemed uncollectible have sharply increased garnishments. In Minnesota, **court-approved seizures have more than tripled over four years. No one tracks garnishments** taking place outside the courts.

When mistakes occur, consumers often must go to court and

prove it. Their money already taken, they typically cannot afford an attorney and must navigate the court system alone. Cases get bogged down while checks bounce and bills go unpaid. Some people, like Tran, are left so destitute that they go hungry.

The process is hardest on the elderly and disabled. They often must repeatedly file paperwork to retrieve government benefits such as Social Security that are legally protected from garnishment.

#30: Court Gets Wrong Address, Tow Truck Gets Right One

Source:

http://www.boston.com/news/special/spotlight_debt/part1/page3.html

News Item:

But for some debtors chased by Norfolk and Commonwealth, it is literally the first they have heard that they are being sued. In several lawsuits examined by Globe reporters, the **two companies provided incorrect addresses to the courts**, with the result that judgments were issued without the knowledge of the debtors. But **finding the right address is seldom a problem for the constables and sheriffs** Norfolk and Commonwealth hire to seize debtors' cars.

#31: Confuse 'Em Then Go For The Court Judgment

Source:
http://www.boston.com/news/special/spotlight_debt/part1/page6.html

News Item:
For Audrey E. Anderson, a 71-year-old retired Wellesley College teacher, dealing with Chad Goldstone's company, Commonwealth Receivables, turned into an annual nightmare, with Commonwealth seizing her car three times - in 2001, 2002, and 2003.

But what the collection firm took from Anderson wasn't just her 1995 Toyota Camry, she said. It was a retiree's sense of independence. Because her car was seized, Anderson had to lean on her 85-year-old husband, Ezra, and friends, in ways she often found humiliating. "When you're a strong person and you have your car taken, that's like losing your right arm," she said. "You can't do anything."

Unlike Joanne Johnson, **Anderson did receive a notice from Framingham District Court to appear for her initial hearing, on a debt of $2,019. But she also received a letter from Commonwealth saying, "Our representatives are willing to work with you on this matter so that your appearance in court may not be necessary."** (Norfolk sends debtors letters with nearly identical language.)

Anderson said she called to negotiate, started making $50 monthly payments, and was **again told she might not need to appear in court. But when she didn't show, Commonwealth won its case against her by default.** And when Anderson missed a payment several months later, Commonwealth, armed with its court judgment, sent constables and a tow truck for her car.

#32: Judges Set Bail at the Amount the Collector Wants

Source:

Harris Meyer in Seattle

http://crosscut.com/2010/12/27/law-justice/20475/Best-of-2010:-Are-local-courts-overstepping-by-helping-bill-collectors-apply-the-screws-/one_page/

News Item:

Janelle Leslie recently called the police to head off a confrontation with her estranged husband. But when the sheriff's deputies arrived, they told her, to her surprise, that they had a warrant for her arrest. When she asked why, all they could tell her was she had failed to obey a court order, which mystified her. At her request, the deputies waited until she got into the squad car to cuff her, so her 12-year-old daughter wouldn't see.

Leslie, 39, spent the night of July 31 in a jail cell, which she shared with three female inmates who were in on drug charges and who, unlike her, had been in jail before. "It was a huge shock," says the soft-spoken mother of three, who answers questions with "yes sir" and "no sir." She found the experience "pretty hurtful and embarrassing."

She was released the next day after posting a $90 bail. **Still not knowing exactly what she was jailed for**, she was told to contact the Yakima County District Court. She did, and learned she had a court date on Aug. 19. After driving four hours to Yakima that day to make the 1:30 hearing, she finally learned that a civil default judgment had been entered against her in 2006 for about $1,000 in unpaid medical debt incurred while she was living in Yakima. A judge subsequently had issued a bench warrant for her arrest because she hadn't appeared at a hearing to examine her finances for collection purposes.

Leslie says she and her children had moved from Yakima to

Alabama in early 2006 and so she **never received notice of the judgment or hearing**. On top of that, the medical bill was for an MRI for her son that **should have been paid in full by the state Medicaid program.**

Leslie's situation is hardly unique. Even though the constitutions of Washington and most other states explicitly prohibit jailing people for debt, Leslie and many other people in Washington and throughout the country are still being incarcerated in civil debt cases. They typically are charged with contempt of court for failure to appear at a hearing.

In many cases, judges order that their bail money be turned over to the collection agency to satisfy their unpaid debt. Sometimes **bail is set at the same amount as the judgment debt, which makes the court look like an arm of the collection agency**.

"We're supplying this big collection tool for collection agencies," says Fred Corbit, senior attorney for the Northwest Justice Project in Seattle. "Creditors get bailed out, and taxpayers are paying a lot to help them in the process."

#33: Judge Said: "Let Me See Your Jewelry."

Source:

http://www.boston.com/news/special/spotlight_debt/part2/page1.html

News Item:

Diane Albertson's experience in court was nothing short of humiliating.

A 50-year-old mother and nursing student, Albertson stood before Judge Thomas Barrett in Brockton District Court on Feb. 7, called to account for a $438 oil bill that she believed, mistakenly, she had paid. She admits she had been sloppy about the matter, missing court dates twice, in the crush of family and school obligations. And after an initial court judgment against her, she sent a check to satisfy the debt, but stopped payment on it.

That made the plaintiff, Stanley Litchfield of Scudder Fuel, angry - and understandably so. The firm had waited more than a year to be paid. But even he was shocked at what the judge did that day.

"Take your rings off," Barrett said, according to the court's audio transcript of the hearing.

"All of my jewelry?" Albertson replied in dismay. "I can't give you my wedding ring."

"Let me see it," Barrett said, ordering her to approach the bench and splay her hands before him. He then told her sternly to remove the other rings, including her diamond and amethyst engagement ring, and her earrings.

"Are you serious?" Albertson asked, near tears.

"We'll hold them until the debt's paid," Barrett said. "Either that or I'll incarcerate you. Do you want me to incarcerate you?"

Albertson handed over her jewelry, keeping only the thin gold band on her left ring finger. A bailiff sealed them in a plastic bag, where they would stay for a month.

Russell Engler, a law professor, called Barrett's behavior "outrageous."

"Litigants are supposed to be able to be heard and be treated with respect," Engler said. "The judge sets the tone for everything."

Barrett declined to be interviewed.

#34: Strip Searched and Sprayed For Lice for Debt Owed to AIG (The Bailout Recipients)

Source:

http://online.wsj.com/article/SB10001424052748704396504576204553811636610.html?KEYWORDS=ENCORE+CAPITAL+GROUP

News Item:

Earlier this year, Vanderburgh County, Ind., Superior Court Judge Robert Pigman asked Indiana's highest court to review the legality of debt-related warrants after **law-enforcement officials complained they can't quickly access arrest orders for dangerous criminals because their computer system is clogged with debt cases.** The Indiana Supreme Court hasn't responded to the request.

In September 2009, Jeffrey Stearns, a concrete-company owner, answered a knock at the door from a Hancock County, Ind., deputy sheriff. The deputy was holding a warrant to arrest Mr. Stearns for not paying $4,024.88 owed to a unit of American International Group Inc. on a loan for his pickup truck.

After being handcuffed in front of his four children, Mr. Stearns, 29 years old, spent two nights in jail, where he said he was strip-searched and sprayed for lice. Court records show he was released after agreeing to pay $1,500 to the loan company. "I didn't even know I was being sued," he said, though he doesn't dispute owing the money. "It's the scariest thing that ever happened to me."

Mr. Stearns said he never got the summons or two orders to show up before a judge that a deputy sheriff said in court filings were delivered to him. Hancock County Sheriff Mark Shepherd couldn't be reached for comment. Mark Herr, an AIG spokesman, declined to comment on Mr. Stearns but said the lending unit was sold in November.

#35: In Jail for $85

Source:

http://www.startribune.com/investigators/95692619.html?elr=KArksUUUoDEy3LGDiO7aiU

News Item:

In January, a judge sentenced a Kenney, Ill., man "to indefinite incarceration" until he came up with $300 toward a lumber yard debt.

"The law enforcement system has unwittingly become a tool of the debt collectors," said Michael Kinkley, an attorney in Spokane, Wash., who has represented arrested debtors. "The debt collectors are abusing the system and intimidating people, and law enforcement is going along with it." Taxpayers foot the bill for arresting and jailing debtors. In many cases, **Minnesota judges set bail at the amount owed.**

In Minnesota, judges have issued arrest warrants for people who owe as little as $85 -- less than half the cost of housing an inmate overnight. Debtors targeted for arrest owed a median of $3,512 in 2009, up from $2,201 five years ago.

One afternoon last spring, Deborah Poplawski, 38, of Minneapolis was digging in her purse for coins to feed a downtown parking meter when she saw the flashing lights of a Minneapolis police squad car behind her. Poplawski, a restaurant cook, assumed she had parked illegally. Instead, she was headed to jail over a $250 credit card debt.

Less than a month earlier, she learned by chance from an employment counselor that she had an outstanding warrant. Debt Equities, a Golden Valley debt buyer, had sued her, but she says nobody served her with court documents. Thanks to interest and fees, Poplawski was now on the hook for $1,138.

Though she knew of the warrant and unpaid debt, "I wasn't equating the warrant with going to jail, because there wasn't criminal activity associated with it," she said. "I just thought it was a civil thing." **She spent nearly 25 hours at the Hennepin County jail.**

A year later, she still gets angry recounting the experience. A male inmate groped her behind in a crowded elevator, she said. Poplawski also was ordered to change into the standard jail uniform -- gray-white underwear and orange pants, shirt and socks -- in a cubicle the size of a telephone booth. She slept in a room with 12 to 16 women and a toilet with no privacy. One woman offered her drugs, she said.

The next day, Poplawski appeared before a Hennepin County district judge. **He told her to fill out the form listing her assets and bank account, and released her. Several weeks later, Debt Equities used this information to seize funds from her bank account.**

"We hear every day about how there's no money for public services," Poplawski said. "But it seems like the collectors have found a way to get the police to do their work."

#36: Consumers Must Show Up But Lawyers Need Not

Source:

http://www.boston.com/news/special/spotlight_debt/part2/page7.html

News Item:

In a system where defaults are rampant, and where debtors in many courts are presumed to owe the money, **some clerks make it part of their job to assist plaintiffs - even those who skip hearings -- in ways that flout court rules**.

It is a common scene in the windowless, basement room in New Bedford District Court, where assistant clerk-magistrate Thomas W. Alfonse often runs overflowing small-claims sessions. **When a plaintiff fails to respond to the call of a lawsuit, Alfonse routinely prompts Joseph McIntyre, New Bedford's lead covering lawyer, to pick up the case - even though, under the rules, such cases should be dismissed.**

During one busy session last fall, Alfonse asked, "Anyone want to answer for Mr. Bakst?" referring to a lawyer not present that day. McIntyre said he would pick up the case. When no one spoke up to cover a Sovereign Bank lawsuit, McIntyre jumped in: "I'll answer for them." Similarly, on a Bank of America case, Alfonse coached, "That's Daniels's office." Again, McIntyre obliged. And when a lesser-known firm, Natco, had its suit called, and no one responded, Alfonse asked McIntyre to represent the no-show plaintiff.

"My incentive is volume," said McIntyre, a former state legislator, in an interview. He answers for up to 10 plaintiffs a day and makes $15 to $20 per case.

The Natco case illustrates two common abuses of the system. First, **the case should have been dismissed when the plaintiff did not appear**. Second, Alfonse violated court rules when he granted McIntyre a postponement, because the lawyer was, not surprisingly, unprepared to try the case.

Clerks routinely grant these delays, called continuances, when plaintiff lawyers say they need time to prepare. Defendants are almost never shown such deference.

Kiriakos Stergiotis and his wife, Phyllis, owners of a pizza shop, who had been sued by Natco, were outraged that the case was postponed: "If they want to bring you to court and they expect you to be there, they should be here too," Phyllis Stergiotis said.

Asked in an interview why he didn't dismiss cases when neither the plaintiff nor its lawyer appeared, Alfonse said, "It's more paper, more court dates. It's better if we work it out today, for everybody."

#37: How They Treat a Soldier with No Arms

Source:

http://www.boston.com/news/special/spotlight_debt/part2/page1.html

News Item:

The line for the metal detector crept slowly at Brockton District Court on the morning of April 12, 2005. Peter Damon waited anxiously. He didn't want to be late.

Finally, he hoped to face down for good the debt collector who had been hounding him and his mother for more than two years over a $980 credit card bill. He'd had to miss his first scheduled hearing in small-claims court a year earlier, and a note in his file explained why: "Phone call from defendant - he is in the Walter Reed Army Medical Center in Washington, D.C., upon return from Iraq and losing both arms."

A lot of things could have gone Damon's way in the wake of that phone call. None did.

The clerk who took the call could have advised Damon that, under federal law, he could delay the case while he recovered.

The court could have challenged the debt collector, Norfolk Financial Corp., about the claim in its lawsuit that Damon was not a soldier - a claim made under penalties of perjury.

And a **clerk should have simply dismissed the case** when Damon, having recovered sufficiently to take a $400 flight home from the hospital, arrived for a hearing in September of 2004, **only to find the collection lawyer unprepared**.

But such simple justice was denied Damon, as it is thousands of other debtors when they come up against the lowest level of the state court system.

The "people's court" has become the collectors' court, a Globe Spotlight Team investigation has found. It is a *de facto* arm of a fast-growing and aggressive industry that has swamped court dockets with lawsuits - cases that often lead to threats of jail for debtors.

Created to provide a low-cost, level playing field for citizens with disputes of $2,000 or less, the small-claims courts have mutated into a system that often ignores individual rights and shows favoritism toward collectors and their lawyers.

#38: "A System in Which It Is Exceedingly Difficult for Individuals to Prevail."

Source:

Robert Berner and Brian Grow, BusinessWeek
http://www.businessweek.com/magazine/content/08_24/b4088072611398.htm

News Item:

What if a judge solicited cases from big corporations by offering them a business-friendly venue in which to pursue consumers who are behind on their bills? What if the judge tried to make this pitch more appealing by teaming up with the corporations' outside lawyers? And what if the same corporations helped pay the judge's salary?

It would, of course, amount to a conflict of interest and cast doubt on the fairness of proceedings before the judge.

Yet that's essentially how one of the country's largest private arbitration firms operates. The National Arbitration Forum (NAF), a for-profit company based in Minneapolis, specializes in resolving claims by banks, credit-card companies, and major retailers that contend consumers owe them money. **Often without knowing it, individuals agree in the fine print of their credit-card applications to arbitrate any disputes over bills rather than have the cases go to court. What consumers also don't know is that NAF, which dominates credit-card arbitration, operates a system in which it is exceedingly difficult for individuals to prevail.**

Some current and former NAF arbitrators say they make decisions in haste—sometimes in just a few minutes—based on scant information and rarely with debtor participation. Consumers who have been through the process complain that NAF spews baffling paperwork and fails to provide the hearings that it promises. Corporations seldom lose. In California, the one state where arbitration results are made public,

creditors win 99.8% of the time in NAF cases that are decided by arbitrators on the merits, according to a lawsuit filed by the San Francisco city attorney against NAF.

"NAF is nothing more than an arm of the collection industry hiding behind a veneer of impartiality," says Richard Neely, a former justice of the West Virginia Supreme Court who as part of his private practice arbitrated several cases for NAF in 2004 and 2005.

NAF presents its service in print and online advertising as quicker and less-expensive than litigation but every bit as unbiased. Its Web site promotes "a fair, efficient, and effective system for the resolution of commercial and civil disputes in America and worldwide."

But internal NAF documents and interviews with people familiar with the firm reveal a different reality. **Behind closed doors, NAF sells itself to lenders as an effective tool for collecting debts.** The point of these pitches is to persuade the companies to use the firm to resolve clashes over delinquent accounts. JPMorgan Chase (JPM) and Bank of America (BAC) are among the large institutions that do so. A September, 2007, NAF PowerPoint presentation aimed at creditors and labeled "confidential" promises "marked increase in recovery rates over existing collection methods." At times, NAF does this kind of marketing with the aid of law firms representing the very creditors it's trying to sign up as clients.

NAF, which is privately held, employs about 1,700 freelance arbitrators—mostly moonlighting lawyers and retired judges—who handle some 200,000 cases a year, most of them concerning consumer debt. Millions of credit-card accounts mandate the use of arbitration by NAF or one of its rivals.

Problem #5: Litigation Has Also Become a Major Money Source for Enforcers

Comment: There's no doubt that the court systems are stretched to the breaking point with debt litigation at the same time that governments are forced to cut budgets.

Not everyone is hurting financially, though. In the following examples, note how bail money is turned over to debt collectors and a cottage industry has grown around seizing assets and being paid handsomely to do so.

#39: Bail Bond Money Was Turned Over to Debt Collector

Source:

Jessica Silver-Greenberg, The Wall Street Journal
http://online.wsj.com/article/SB10001424052748704396504576204553811636610.html?KEYWORDS=ENCORE+CAPITAL+GROUP

News Item:

Some lawmakers, judges and regulators are trying to rein in the U.S. debt-collection industry's use of arrest warrants to recoup money owed by borrowers who are behind on credit-card payments, auto loans and other bills.

More than a third of all U.S. states allow borrowers who can't or won't pay to be jailed. Judges have signed off on more than 5,000 such warrants since the start of 2010 in nine counties with a total population of 13.6 million people, according to a tally by The Wall Street Journal of filings in those counties. Nationwide figures aren't known because many courts don't keep track of warrants by alleged offense. In interviews, 20 judges across the nation said the number of borrowers threatened with arrest in their courtrooms has surged since the financial crisis began.

Some judges elsewhere are issuing fewer debt-related arrest warrants because law-enforcement officials complained those cases gobble up resources needed to pursue violent offenders.

In September, the Illinois Department of Financial and Professional Regulation issued an order seeking to revoke the license of Easy Money Express Inc. The Paducah, Ky., payday lender won arrest warrants against at least four customers. One spent five days in a Carbondale, Ill., jail last March after failing to pay a $275 debt, court filings show. The lender "exploited the court system to obtain the arrest and incarceration of its customers," said Sue Hofer, a spokeswoman for the agency. The company declined to comment but is fighting the state's proposed ban.

In one of those cases, Emmie Nichols, 26 years old, was arrested in June at her mother's house after lawyers for Capital One Financial Corp. won an arrest warrant against her for skipping a court hearing about $1,159.87 she owed on a credit card from the company. **The $500 bond that freed Ms. Nichols from the county jail was turned over to Capital One as a partial payment of the debt,** court filings show. A Capital One spokeswoman declined to comment on Ms. Nichols. Some judges are worried that the jump in debt-related arrest warrants is creating a modern-day version of debtors' prison. The practice ended in 1833 after decades of controversy, since borrowers owing as little as 60 cents could be held indefinitely in squalid jails until they paid off their debt.

#40: $5,600 in Storage Charges for a Car

Source:
http://www.boston.com/news/special/spotlight_debt/part1/page7.html

News Item:

Losing a car is bad enough. But losing a car, a house, and a job was what faced Michaelyn S. Rackley and her husband, Raheem R. Weldon, in 2001, after Norfolk Financial filed a lawsuit against Rackley - and sent notice of the suit to the wrong address. She lives in Athol. Norfolk sued her at an address in Waltham.

Unlike Chad Goldstone, Daniel Goldstone often goes after debtors' homes, as well as their cars. Real estate records examined by the Globe show that, over the last four years, Norfolk has put liens on more than 1,000 homes throughout the state. Once a lien is placed on a home, it cannot be sold or even refinanced unless the lien holder is paid.

Norfolk filed its lawsuit against Rackley on May 1, 2001, for a $543 credit card debt. **Court records show that the notice sent to Waltham was returned undelivered** - which should have prompted the Waltham District Court to demand a correct address from the collector, or dismiss the lawsuit. Nonetheless, on Aug. 13, 2001, Norfolk won an **automatic judgment against Rackley - because Rackley did not appear for a hearing she knew nothing about**.

Then last summer, Norfolk first came after Rackley's car, and then her home.

The Worcester County deputy sheriffs and a tow truck hauled away her 1998 Subaru Forester in June. As a consequence, Rackley had to quit her job delivering newspapers for the Worcester Telegram & Gazette.

In July, Daniel Goldstone placed a lien on the couple's Athol home. In October, Rackley had no choice but to pay off the debt - $1,038, with accumulated interest - when the couple went to refinance their home.

But Rackley never got her Subaru back. After it was seized, **the storage charges mounted daily - all the way to $5,600** by October. In December, Direnzo Towing & Recovery of Millbury sold the vehicle to recoup its costs, according to the Worcester County sheriff's office.

#41: "Don't Argue With Us."

Source:

http://www.boston.com/news/special/spotlight_debt/part3/page2.html

News Item:

Marie LoConte had her close encounter with constables shortly after midnight on July 28, 2004, when her doorbell rang.

LoConte, 41, made her way down the stairs from her second-floor apartment and found three men wearing blue uniforms and badges. "They looked like police officers. I thought they were," LoConte said. One of them, she recalls, was tapping his nightstick in the palm of his hand while another informed her they were there to seize her 1997 Ford Thunderbird for an unpaid credit card debt.

"Don't argue with us," she heard him say.

Terrified, LoConte said, she called Taunton police, who offered little sympathy. The constable brandishing the nightstick was playing by the rules, she says she was told, as long as he didn't hit her with it. "I didn't sleep all that night. I couldn't stop crying. I was shaking," LoConte said.

LoConte is disabled as a result of lupus and Crohn's Disease. She lost her cleaning business more than a decade ago, and, by 2000, had stopped making payments on a $430 Providian credit card balance. She wound up paying $1,758, draining her savings and borrowing from a friend, to erase the debt and get her car back.

Of that, $158 went to the tow lot, which kept her car for a day, and $800 to the constables, dispatched by Sorenson's firm. To ransom the car, LoConte had to drive 70 miles to Sorenson's office in Chelmsford to pay her bill, then another 55 miles to a Bridgewater tow lot.

For Jeanmarie Fitzpatrick, the constable's visit was even more costly. An $800 constable's fee would have seemed a bargain to her.

When Dorsey, the former bar manager turned constable, arrived at her door last Dec. 14, he demanded $1,250 in fees for seizing her 2000 Dodge Neon.

Fitzpatrick, a 37-year-old single mother who lives in South Boston's D Street public housing project, was about to drive her three children to school when Dorsey drove up and blocked her car. Fitzpatrick figured it must be something to do with unpaid parking tickets; she said she had no idea there were court judgments against her for two delinquent credit card accounts, totaling $3,800. That's because Norfolk Financial Corp., the debt collector who sued Fitzpatrick, had **given the court the wrong address**. She says she was never notified of the lawsuit, and a Globe check of court and public records shows she's right.

"They went out of their way to find my car but they didn't go through the trouble to find my address" to notify me about the lawsuit, Fitzpatrick said. "That's what kills me."

Dorsey, she said, turned aside her tearful plea that he wait to take her car until she could drop the children at school.

Dorsey's fee for having her car hauled away: $625. But **since he was holding two pieces of legal paper for taking just one car, he demanded $1,250.** The car was sold at auction for just $1,000, even though it had a resale value of about $4,000.

#42: Fee Went From $25 to $900

Source:

http://www.boston.com/news/special/spotlight_debt/part3/page1.html

News Item:

They have the power to take your car, your money, and sometimes your freedom. And they bring some uncommon credentials to the job. Consider these resume highlights:

Kenneth J. Dorsey: Manager of a Jamaica Plain gin mill. Ran illegal gaming operation. Busted by Boston Police. Rifle and shotgun confiscated. Guilty plea, 1994.

Kevin J. Dalton: Plymouth County deputy sheriff until 2001. Fired after State Police probe into alleged shakedown of a company seeking a contract with the sheriff's department, an accusation he denies.

Constance M. Sorenson: Filed for bankruptcy in 2003 with $47,000 in delinquent credit card debt. Fined for punching a woman in the mouth outside a bar. Arrest warrant pending for failure to pay $100 fine in another case. Along with that baggage, Sorenson, Dalton, and Dorsey also carry badges - as officers in the murkiest backwater of the Massachusetts law enforcement community. They earn their keep as constables, independent operators appointed by cities and towns to serve court papers and execute court orders.

In Boston alone there are 186 of them, and Mayor Thomas M. Menino has given arrest powers to every one, including Dorsey and 87 others with criminal arrest records for offenses including firearms violations, indecent assault and battery on a child, and impersonating a police officer. **Seven have been appointed in spite of guilty verdicts**, among them one convicted twice in the last four years of beating his wife.

Constables are an odd, anachronistic leftover from colonial days. **No**

training is required, no oversight is provided, and no state agency keeps track of their identities, much less their numbers - an estimated 1,500 to 2,000 statewide.

Yet many among them, including Dorsey, Dalton, and Sorenson, are foot soldiers for the most aggressive debt collectors in Massachusetts. They make their money by night, or at first light, with a frightening thump on the door, seizing cars by the thousands from intimidated debtors who have missed, or ignored, court orders to pay their creditors.

Most constables prefer to knock politely during daylight hours to deliver subpoenas and the like for their $35 or $40 fee.

But their more aggressive colleagues do much, much better than that, thanks to a 1990 amendment to state law that **allows them to charge whatever they like for auto seizures. The result is price-gouging: Constables charge debtors between $600 and $900 to accompany the tow truck that arrives to hook a car. The fee used to be capped at $25.**

When debtors cannot raise the cash to pay the debt and the seizure fees, their cars are sold at auction. Here again the constables are part of the game: **Proceeds of the auction are split among the constable, the tow lot, and the creditor.** Almost always ignored, the Globe found, is a state law requiring that the first $700 of the sale proceeds be returned to debtors.

Take the case of Marlene Cote, of Leominster, who last December filed for bankruptcy - a step that legally protects assets from seizure. Or so Cote thought, until the evening of Jan. 13, when two deputy sheriffs banged on her door at 8:30 p.m. and said they were seizing her 11-year-old Jeep.

By Cote's account, the deputies were undeterred when she showed them her bankruptcy filing. They even threatened to arrest her when she stood between the tow truck and her vehicle.

Cote's debt, an old $300 bill from a local dentist, barely topped $600 with accumulated interest. The fee charged by the deputies added another $600. And the towing company wanted $310. The total - for a car that could not legally be seized - was $1,530.56.

When the Globe first raised Cote's case with Deputy Turco in mid-March, he acknowledged that the deputy sheriffs should have checked with his office when they were presented with the bankruptcy documents. According to his office records, Cote's car was returned within a few days when the error was discovered.

In fact, the car was still being held, two months after it was towed away, by Direnzo Towing & Recovery, which had added another $1,200 in storage fees in the interim.

Finally, at the end of March, Cote's car was returned and all the charges were waived. But Cote paid dearly for the episode as she struggled to regain her financial footing.

During the 10 weeks she had to get by without her Jeep, Cote said, she spent between $600 and $800 to commute by taxi to her $8-an-hour job as a cashier at a Kohl's department store in Leominster. During that period, she also had to abandon a second job, caring for mental health patients in group homes in Athol and Gardner.

It felt to her, as to many who lose their cars to unpaid debts, like a prison term for a traffic offense. And such penalties are far from rare: A review of Worcester sheriff's office records showed numerous instances of debt collectors engaging deputy sheriffs to seize cars from people with small unpaid debts. Often, the fees associated with seizure doubled or even tripled the amount of the original debt.

#43: 11-Cent Bill Ballooned to $4,000

Source:

Good Morning America
http://abcnews.go.com/GMA/story?id=4358702&page=1

News Item:

Like the phoenix that rises from the ashes, so does so-called zombie debt. A consumer may think it's dead, but it keeps coming back to haunt.

"Zombie debt is a phrase to describe all debt that a consumer had forgotten about or never even owed that comes back to haunt them," said Joseph Mauro, of the Consumer Protection Attorney.

Nancy Rose was tormented for years as collection agencies hassled her about debt that wasn't even hers. More than a decade ago Rose had her identity stolen and since then debt collectors have been stealing her peace of mind.

"It is a nightmare. It won't go away," Rose said. "I had knots in my stomach. I was on the phone for hours."

Rose reported a fraudulent $5,000 charge and still the bill collectors were relentless. When she refused to pay, they went after her credit rating. **Each time she cleared her name with one agency, the cycle started up again because her debt had been sold to a different bill collector.**

Rose finally sued the persistent collection agency for fraud five years ago. Rose was awarded $40,000.

Her experience isn't an isolated one.

When George Lovelock missed a Verizon bill for 11 cents, it ballooned into $4,000 seven years later.

Lovelock said the collector backed off when he made it clear that he knew his rights.

"If they are going after me, someone who has the resources to fight them, what are they doing to people who don't understand their rights?" he said.

"I think what I did was make them aware that I was aware," Lovelock said.

#44: $260 Grew To $5,818

Source:

http://www.startribune.com/investigators/97231639.html

News Item:

Bonnie Hanson of Rockford, once co-signed for a Best Buy credit card used by her daughter, who defaulted in the late 1990s. The debt grew even though Hanson wrote a check to pay it off.

Sept. 5, 1997 Hanson pays off the defaulted card.

June 30, 1999 An unpaid balance of $260 shows up on the card, unknown to Hanson.

March 31, 2001 Account is written off as a loss by bank that issued the card for Best Buy.

April 21, 2001 Bank sells the debt to Sherman Financial Group of New York, which resumes collection efforts by phone.

June 25, 2004 The debt on the closed account grows to $2,747. Court records don't explain the increase.

Oct. 5, 2006 Sherman Financial sells the debt to Dakota Bluff Financial LLC, a debt buyer associated with the Messerli & Kramer law firm of Minneapolis.

July 12, 2007 A Messerli lawyer signs court papers against Bonnie Hanson trying to collect the ballooned debt of $2,747, plus another $3,071 in fees, costs and interest.

Jan. 18, 2008 Hennepin County District Court enters a judgment against Bonnie Hanson and her daughter for $5,818. Hanson's paycheck later is garnished for repayment.

June 9, 2008 A Faegre & Benson attorney helping Hanson at no cost writes to the Messerli firm questioning its conduct in the case. The garnishment soon ends and the money is returned.

Part Two: What Do We Do About the Problem?

These news items are from all across the country, reported by a variety of organizations, yet they represent only a portion of what my files contain. Given the level of abuse, what are possible solutions?

Should we ban debt collectors?

That is a bad idea. Of course, I'm biased because I'm a debt collector. Still, you don't have to be a debt collector to see that it serves a valuable function in our society. Just as we all pay more when people shoplift, walking away with something they didn't pay for, we all will pay more if other people can walk away from their debts with no consequences. Not only will credit become less available—or unavailable—to many more people, but those that do get credit will pay more to cover the cost of uncollectible debt.

Should we let the industry regulate itself?

Certain professions have avoided full governmental regulation by creating SROs, or Self-Regulatory Organizations. Examples are the National Association of Realtors and the American Medical Association. Would that work for the debt-collection industry?

Maybe, but judging by industry organizations already in place, it's not looking good. Consider the following:

- CNN.com interviewed Rozanne Andersen, who at the time was General Counsel at ACA International, a debt-collection trade group. She said that harassing phone calls and the aggressive behavior were "absolutely unacceptable," yet she went on to say that about 10 percent of debt collectors are rogue and "can do tremendous harm."[3]

  The industry's own trade group says ten percent! Let's assume for a moment that the trade group is not low-balling the figure.

---

[3] http://www.cnn.com/2009/CRIME/08/21/debt.collection/index.html

One Federal Trade Commission report mentioned an estimate that in 2007 there were 152,000 people employed in just one part of the debt-collection industry.[4] Therefore by the trade group's own estimate **we have roughly 15,000 rogue people in the system, capable of doing "tremendous harm."**

- Valerie Hayes is the current General Counsel for ACA International, and she also oversees the complaint-resolution program. She said: **"There is no hard data to back up the claim that debt buyers are filing unsubstantiated lawsuits. "It's hard to solve the problem when you're not sure what the problem is.**" [5]
- *Text from FTC Annual Report:* "In October 2010, the FTC reached a settlement agreement with collector Allied Interstate, Inc. ("Allied"), one of the nation's largest debt collectors. The Commission alleged that Allied continued collection efforts even after consumers told the company that they did not owe the debt, without verifying the accuracy of the disputed information or otherwise having a reasonable basis for representing that the consumers owed the debt. The FTC further alleged that Allied violated the FDCPA and Section 5 of the FTC Act by making improper harassing phone calls to consumers (using abusive language or calling many times a day for weeks or months); making repeated calls to third parties seeking to locate a consumer; revealing alleged debts to third parties without the consumer's consent or court permission; and threatening legal action against consumers that it did not intend to take. Under the settlement agreement, Allied paid a $1.75 million civil penalty

---

[4] *Collecting Consumer Debts: The Challenges of Change*, Federal Trade Commission workshop report.February, 2009, page 13.
[5] http://www.startribune.com/investigators/97231649.html?page=2&c=y

and agreed to stop collection efforts on disputed debts in the future unless and until it conducts a reasonable investigation and verifies the debt. In addition, the agreement bars Allied from violating the FDCPA or from engaging in the types of conduct the complaint alleged violated the FTC Act.[6]
Nevertheless, (as of early April 2011) ACA International still lists Allied Interstate as a member, even though the ACA International "Code of Ethics" clearly prohibits member companies from engaging in the acts listed by the FTC against Allied Interstate.[7]

- *Text from FTC Annual Report:* In March 2011, the Commission announced a settlement agreement with collector West Asset Management, Inc. ("WAM"), resulting in a $2.8 million civil penalty, the largest civil penalty ever obtained by the FTC in a debt collection case. The complaint alleged WAM violated the FDCPA by calling consumers and third parties repeatedly with intent to harass or annoy, and by revealing debts to third parties and calling them for reasons other than to obtain location information about the consumer. In addition, the Commission alleged that WAM engaged in deception in violation of the FTC Act by materially misrepresenting to consumers that WAM was a law firm, it would bring civil action or criminal prosecution against consumers who failed to pay, and nonpayment would result in the seizure, garnishment, attachment, or sale of consumers' properties or wages, or their arrest or imprisonment. The FTC further alleged WAM engaged in unfairness in violation of the FTC Act by debiting consumers' financial accounts or charging their credit cards without their express, informed consent.

---

[6]*Federal Trade Commission Annual Report 2011: Fair Debt Collection Practices Act*, pages 11-12.
[7]Code of Ethics and Code of Operations of ACA International, Adopted July 25, 2007.

Nevertheless, (as of early April 2011) ACA International still lists West Asset Management as a member, even though the ACA International "Code of Ethics" clearly prohibits member companies from engaging in the acts listed by the FTC against West Asset Management.[8]

It seems obvious that something would have to change for the industry to be able to regulate itself.

I recommend another option

I believe the solution does not lie in just passing more laws. That may make lawmakers feel like they accomplished something, but let's remember that many of the abuses I've outlined are already illegal.

Instead, let's look at the five problems I identified above, and actions I recommend be taken to solve them.

Problem #1: Some industry players—including some of the biggest ones—are simply not worried about current rules, or the consequences of violating them.

Proposal: Increase the penalty for violations of debt-collection rules from the current $1,000 to $10,000 for each violation.

Background: Given the examples in this document it is clear that current financial penalties are not a sufficient deterrent to illegal behavior. Not only should the penalties be substantially raised, but the proceeds of penalties should first go toward strengthening supervision and enforcement.

Proposal: Allow consumers to record telephone calls from collection agencies.

In California, Florida, and ten other states it's currently a crime for a citizen to record a call without the other party's consent. With respect to debt-collection calls it's critical that victims be

[8]Code of Ethics and Code of Operations of ACA International, Adopted July 25, 2007.

able to document the nature of the calls they receive, so their complaints have some degree of validation and do not fall into the "he said/she said" category.

Proposal: Require an annual compliance audit for all collection agencies.

Background: This audit would be in the form of a report from each collection to the licensing authority. It would indicate the amount of training each collector received in the prior period, and also the results of an annual criminal background check on each collector.

Problem #2: It is too easy to become a debt collector, no matter how checkered the person's background might be.

Proposal: Require all collection agencies to be licensed.

Background: Most states require beauticians to be licensed, but not debt collectors. Without licensing of both individual collectors and collection agencies, it's far too easy for these companies to abuse thousands of customers for months until they're caught, only to scatter and regroup elsewhere in order to do it all over again.

Proposal: Require all individual collectors to be licensed.

Background: Licensing would involve requiring a clean criminal record of the applicant. In addition, licensing would require both an initial training period and ongoing training of collectors with respect to federal and state laws regarding the collection of consumer debt. Just as plumbers and doctors can lose their license for documented infractions, the system should be similar for debt collectors.

Problem #3: Some debt collectors pursue ancient debts that have been dormant for years and in fact are older than the statute of limitations.

Proposal: Ban all collection activities on debt that is older than the applicable statute of limitations.

Background: Our criminal justice system already recognizes the concept of a statute of limitations even for violent crimes. The thought is that after a sufficient number of years, even unsolved violent crimes should be archived for no further action.

If that makes sense for criminal violations it makes even more sense for non-violent, civil violations like defaulting on a debt.

Problem #4: It's Far Too Easy for Major Corporations to Sue for Debt Collection

Proposal: Require collection agencies to provide clear and understandable history of debt.

Background: This would mean that the original creditor and each subsequent holder of the debt must retain and pass on to the next holder all communications from the consumer concerning the debt and information about all known disputes. It also means that consumers must be notified in writing that they can receive a copy of the history within 60 days of their written request, and that all collection activities must be suspended until that request is fulfilled.

Proposal: Raise the requirements necessary to file a lawsuit on credit card debt.

Background: Require that any attorney or law firm representing a collection agency must verify that the agency is in compliance with state licensing requirements, that the debt is not time-barred (i.e., past the statute of limitations), and that the agency possesses proof of the debt—not just a name, amount, and Social Security number.

Proposal: Require proof of personal service before litigation

Background: Require that consumers be served notice of any

collection lawsuit in a manner that provides proof of the delivery of the summons. It is not good enough to send a first-class letter and assume it arrived. Proof might involve certified mail with signature required; in cases where that mail was not picked up, then personal delivery of the summons would be necessary.

In addition to the summons delivery, a clear explanation must be delivered in writing. That document would explain clearly and conspicuously the reasons for the court hearing, the consequences of not appearing, and a way to contact the court to request a postponement.

Problem #5: Litigation Has Become a Major Money Source for Enforcers

Proposal: Revamp the fees charged borrowers by those involved in the system.

Background: When the justice system sees fit to seize cars or imprison people, it becomes a travesty of justice to pile on so many fees that those people have little chance of paying them back. It's unconscionable for badge-wearing constables to gouge people $900 to tow a car, or for tow-truck operators to charge people many thousands to store a car. It's also unrealistic for sheriffs to imprison people—thus taking away their earning capacity—and then charge them high daily jail rates.

A schedule of fees should be set and periodically reviewed by an entity that has no financial interest in the outcome, similar to how utility and insurance rates are reviewed.

If You Would Like to Help

We are working to reform the broken debt-collection system across all 50 states, but it's a monumental task. These reforms are a direct threat to debt collectors, lawyers, and others for whom profit is much more important than principle. They will do everything they can to stop this effort.

Here are two ways you can help:

1. Go to www.stopthesecriminals.com and sign the petition. I will personally deliver the petition signatures to Washington, along with stories of abuse (the website has a section for people to document their stories).

2. Contact me at: reform@billbartmann.com and tell me how you think you could help. I'm open to any ideas you may have.

This fight is winnable. Our country has a history of implementing reforms to protect its citizens. I recognize that sometimes it has taken too long, or the reforms may have not been strong enough. Let's not lament that, but instead let's work to correct the current injustices and create a debt-collection system that demands nothing less than the treatment of borrowers with dignity and respect.

Bill Bartmann

About Bill Bartmann

Bill Bartmann is Founder and Chairman of CFS II, a debt-collection company based in Tulsa, Oklahoma.

The son of a janitor and house-cleaner, Bill put himself through college and law school by working nights at a slaughterhouse. Bill became a union steward for *Local 150 of the Amalgamated Meat Cutters and Butcher Workmen of North America, AFL-CIO.* He organized a strike to demand benefits for part-time employees and was successful.

Bill's consumer advocacy started 26 years ago after graduating from law school. His first clients were individuals being sued by debt collectors. He won notoriety in the press for his aggressive defense of clients via the Uniform Consumer Credit Code.

In 1986, Bill and Kathy Bartmann got into the debt-collection business almost by accident. They were deeply in debt due to the failure of an oil-related business after the price of oil plummeted. Bill was looking for a way to feed his family and stumbled upon a portfolio of defaulted loans that the government was auctioning. It was the first such auction in America and Bill "won" the portfolio as the only bidder. He used borrowed money to win it.

Soon Bill and Kathy were making phone calls from their kitchen table to customers who owed money. Because they personally had been hounded by predatory debt collectors in the past, Bill and Kathy vowed they would never treat customers the way they had been mistreated. They treated customers with dignity and respect, and quickly discovered that most of those customers wanted to find a way to pay back their debts.

Bill and Kathy were able to make a small profit on that portfolio and repeat the process. After a while they paid off their own debts and realized they were onto something, so they formed a company.

In the years since 1986, Bill and his team have successfully settled debt for more than 4.5 million Americans. They accomplished it not by employing a "boiler room" of commissioned, strong-arm debt collectors, but by creating a family-friendly staff of salaried people who would help customers to solve their financial problems. Here is a sample of third-party commentary:

- *The Nilson Report*, an industry trade journal, called Bill's company the "largest, best-trained, and most profitable collection operation in the world."
- Received the U.S. Better Business Bureau's *Torch Award* for ethics in the marketplace.
- Recognized by *Working Woman* magazine as "One of the top 100 Best Companies for Working Mothers". (This was not a yoga school but instead a debt-collection company.)
- Acknowledged by *Business Week* magazine as "One of the Top Ten Family-Oriented Businesses in America."
- *Fortune* magazine said: "Bill Bartmann is a Populist Capitalist. He put a seedy and inefficient industry on the road to respectability."

Though the world has changed a lot in the last quarter century, the CFS II approach to collecting debt has not changed at all. It's still firmly rooted in the insistence that customers must always be treated with dignity and respect.